The Mermaid Queen

Anthony Thomas Langley

Copyright © Anthony Thomas Langley 2015
This book is sold subject to the condition that it shall not, by way of trade or otherwise, be lent, resold, hired out, or otherwise circulated without the publisher's prior consent in any form of binding or cover other than that in which it is published and without a similar condition including this condition being imposed on the subsequent publisher.
The moral right of Anthony Thomas Langley has been asserted.
ISBN-13: 978-1508717362
ISBN-10: 1508717362

DEDICATION

To two people who believed in me - Simon Usher (former artistic director of Riverside Studios Theatre and Idola Martinez (Spanish Judge)

ACKNOWLEDGMENTS

Queen of Heaven - Mhuire.

FOREWORD

This epic poem was written in 1979 and had its first reading by the Sphinx Drama Group in the Riverside Studios in 1984, in which it was very well received.

Soon to be performed as a contemporary ballet with folk-classical music.

It was first published in 1984, and just 120 copies were printed – most of which were sold to top bookshops in the West End of London.

THE MERMAID QUEEN

(PRELUDE)

Crash!

A splintered brain, anguished cry of pain;

Split wooden mouths gaping, twisted shocked expressions.

Seems a trembling shock has forced a hole in the soul of humanity.

Dreams lie shattered with porcelain pieces

As spattered feet crunch the life out of time.

Muted screams fall on numbed eardrums.

Unwaiting death appears out of tune with the mass of swaying bodies

Whose orchestral hands flail, and grope the blanket gloom,

Portraying a gruesome scene of self-preservation.

Desperately, I grab, and hug the belly of an umbilical shell;

And in a symbiotic embrace make love with the cord around the waist.

The crows surge forward to proclaim me king,

Not allowing for abdication as they rush me along in waves of

Unbridled emotion.

But fate in jealous rage decides that this will be another page

Of unwritten history,

And with a bellowing roar flings all through the castrated bowels Into oblivion.

Down, down I fall, into the seething turbulence, clinging tenaciously to the battered hope, as demon luck plays its icy hand upon the slope of moral fortitude. But fortune with concusses force maintains the equilibrium by levelling the bent ears of impassive justice with a coarse, shattering cry of "Not guilty!" and thrusts me into the waters of clear conscience to wrestle with the Id, and do battle with dazed reality.

Timeless strangulation tightens its hold around hope, causing the seeds of despair to take root and create a deep, deep sleep precipitating a suicidal leap into the unfathomable abyss.

I awaken to tinkling music, and dazzling bursts of light, illuminating, dancing, grinning Nereids.

Their spindly arms sway a balletic, tendrilled welcome in unison with multi-coloured octopus-type plants.

Flaxen-coloured almond eyed maidens ripple a transparent blue mirror.

One with red hair and scarlet costume sits on a moss-covered stone strumming a harp. The entrancing, endearing music magnetically pulls me towards her.

She rises, runs away and beckons to follow.

Black peaty mud squelches beneath my hands as I claw my way after her. Though I seem to be going the faster, the distance between us does not lessen.

Exhausted, I fall on top of a mound embedded with coloured stones and beaded weeds.

A haunting, musical voice echoes in my weary head.

"Awaken, Adonis the beautiful, awaken. I am Queen Elena – welcome to our world."

A silvery, slender hand softly brushes my hair, and a perfume kiss caresses my cheek.

Another hand holds out a golden-shaped object.

"Here, take this and it will refresh you – it is life."

I eat the nectar from the hive, and feel the love food touch my soul into an awareness of a beautiful lady with mystical charms, and long, fragrant, plaited yellow hair bedecked with a silver-jewelled tiara.

She is dressed in a Greco-Roman type costume, exposing the magnificence of her bronzed, moist, athletic legs.

Her lips seem to ghost waves of aesthetically beautiful sounds as she speaks.

"Because of your beauty, sensitivity and vision, you have been chosen to journey with us on the Voyage of Life and Death."

Her aquamarine eyes take on a soulful expression.

"We are deeply concerned. You must take a message back from us that your world will be totally destroyed from germ and chemical warfare, unless the powerful nations use their economic might to establish social justice, and defend truth.

There are nihilists from both left and right of the political spectrum who believe in a pre-emptive strike.

"You task will be to unite all moderate forces.

"Women, because of their empathy, compassion, and intuitive powers, could determine the final outcome.

"The 'Super Powers' should collaborate on combating famine, disease and inequality, jointly develop the 'Space Programme' and a feasible laser beam defence system.

"Create a new awareness that survival is dependent upon symbiotic coexistence, and a mutual respect for common humanity.

"Wars leave a painful scar on the soul of humanity. The misery and suffering they cause is mirrored in the eyes of the innocents. The barbaric slaughter of intelligent, beneficial sea-creatures should also be condemned.

"Unnecessary destruction of vegetation, animal and human life for selfish, expedient economic reasons will prove to be detrimental, and result in self-inflicted chastisements. Your people must learn to affiliate with nature – not destroy it.

"They must learn to perceive the creative life source – the richness and beauty of the spiritual dimension – the power of love and goodness," Elena smiles.

"When you go back to earth some will say that I am a figment of your imagination.

"I would say to them that imagination can be the mirror of a true reality – the womb from which futuristic ideas are born."

Elena pauses, then kneels and puts a hand on my shoulder.

"Do not fret, Adonis – you are not dead – Death is but an attitude of mind.

"You are a Libran – a guardian of the scales of justice. You must maintain the equilibrium.

"The journey which we are about to embark on will not be easy. Demons and evil forces will try to stop us, but do not fear; my warrior maidens will protect you, and fight to the last one to ensure that you get back."

Elena pauses, looks around, then clasps my hand.

"Come, it is time to go."

We climb up a rope ladder onto an Ark-type ship.

Elena beckons me to lie on a hammock of matted rushes and coloured ferns.

She lies on an adjacent hammock, leans down and picks up a melon-type object.

She gestures me to bite it. We eat it together.

I find myself drifting into a sublime state of relaxation, and listen to the urgent groaning of the ship locked in intercourse with the embracing waves.

I watch the honey trickle from Elena's soft lips and flow sweetly like a virgin in a mountain stream.

Her hair glistens when I touch it, reflecting a bright sheen of grace.

She murmurs, "Come, come my loved one – into

the land of uncharted fantasy."

The floodgates of my mind burst open and I am thrust into a sea of ecstasy.

Then begins a gentle rocking, heaving, locking of twin souls breathing coals of passionate fire weaving higher and higher until it all culminates in a climactic shudder.

With a smooth thrust the ship moves into a chasm called the 'Fountain of Youth'.

Nymph maidens dance, and joyously weep silver tears which cascade into layers of foamy spray, and become a waterfall.

Siren voices sing a song of the sea.

Elena sings in harmony with them.

Her golden hair blows free, embraced by mermaid spirits in the wind.

A tall red-haired mermaid, a platinum blonde and dainty brunette perform a circular dance. Afterwards, they bring platters of food and a pitcher of exquisite dark red wine.

Elena introduces the tall red-haired one as 'Muireadnesi the Fearless', the blonde as 'Luminae the Thinker', and the dainty one as 'Marah, Daughter of the Night."

I am embraced by the three mermaids, who smile, wish me good luck and then exit.

Elena calls me over to the side of the Ark, and points.

"We shall soon be reaching the land of sleep. Over there is Hades. Do not be afraid. You will be protected."

Soon, storm-clouds appear. The ship is covered in total darkness. The sea becomes heavy, making the Ark moan and lurch.

The storm grows fiercer, buffeting the sea maidens who desperately cling to the sides trying to keep the Ark on an even keel.

The warrior maidens crouch behind shell shields, trident spears at the ready, and sing a battle hymn.

Their mother-of-pearl bracelets glint in the darkness, reminiscent of flickering church candles.

Whoosh! The Ark is lifted suddenly by a tidal wave.

A scaly monster with three towering heads, saucer-shaped eyes and nostrils breathing fire appears.

"It is Tethra," Elena murmurs. She stands aloft and shouts, "Achaea, Achae, Oreechue."

The monster's heads sway inquisitively. Elena calls again.

The sea breaks, and a shoal of dolphins appears.

They cut through the water like black bullets, shrieking as they hit the monster with tremendous force.

Its three heads lash the water and frantically try to bite, and burn.

The dolphins encircle, and attack again.

Elena calls out instructions in accentuated tones.

The dolphins hit the monster three times – it topples over, fumes with rage, and then slowly submerges.

The water becomes murky; a wailing sound can be heard.

Red-eyed green demons peer through the darkness.

They advance towards the Ark.

The mermaids rush to battle, fling their trident spears, and inflict electric shock waves upon the enemy.

Two of the demons manage to climb aboard.

Their slimy stench fouls the air, and makes it difficult to breathe.

One crawls towards me, mumbling strange sounds, and gesticulating with its claw-like hands.

I fasten the two pieces of matted straw into a cross, and thrust it into the demon's face.

It cowers, and then falls backwards.

The other demon snarls, and spits abuse at Elena.

She raises her curved coral sword aloft, and with one mighty lightning strike, she decapitates the demon.

As it falls its outstretched claws rip into Elena's flesh – she burns off the embedded claws with her sword.

The creature's head rolls crazily across the deck.

Anxiously watching Elena, I am unaware that the other demon has sneaked up behind me.

It jumps and knocks me down, snarling, biting, scratching.

It seizes me by the throat. I try to push it away, but my hands keep sliding off its scaly skin.

The demon tightens its grip, causing numbness and paralysis.

I hear a humming sound followed by a dull thud.

The demon jerks backwards, gasps, and then falls limp.

A triangular object protrudes from its back.

Luminae, holding a whalebone crossbow, kicks the demon away, reaches down and picks me up.

She snarls and speaks softly, "I was just in time."

Her luminous eyes glow in the darkness.

The other demon's decapitated head bounces towards us.

Luminous legs become a fish-tail. She whacks the head with tremendous force. It zooms away like a cannonball.

Her face takes on an anxious expressing as more demons swarm over the sides.

She ushers me to the back of the ship, and puts me under Muireadnesi's protection.

The whizzing and humming of arrows fill the air with weird music as the battle intensifies.

Some of the mermaids collapse from exhaustion and injury.

Piles of bodies litter the deck of the Ark.

"Onnaghh!" A terrifying grumbling sound emanates from the sea. The Ark lists heavily, throwing some of the mermaids and demons, locked in deadly combat, over the side.

A giant horned creature appears.

"It is the evil one," shouts Muireadnesi.

She and a dozen of her warriors kneel, and draw diamond-shaped stones from their pouches.

They put the stones into their slingshots.

Muireadnesi gives the order to fire.

The stones fly, and hit the horned creature's head.

Its skin sizzles, and becomes scorched.

Its face turns whitish-blue.

Eel-like red eyed snakes emerge from the sea,

And with their long necks provide a protective shield.

The horned creature advances, and leers down at the Ark.

It seems the mermaids are on the brink of defeat.

Elena calls to Luminae, who removes a fish-shaped jewelled studded trumpet from a golden triangular casket.

She fights her way across, and hands the trumpet

to Elena. Elena puts the tail end to her mouth, and blows.

A million sounds of varying pitch and tone gush forth.

A blinding flash of light is followed by a loud crack.

Thousands of fluorescent-faced tiny winged creatures fall from the sky, carrying a silvery thread net.

The net falls gently onto the sea,

trapping the horned creature and demons.

The sprite-like creatures buzz back and forth,

like a swarm of bees. They haul the net away,

and gradually disappear from view.

The rest of the demons on the Ark scatter, and try to get away,

But many are destroyed by the mermaids.

Next morning I awake to a sad lament.

News comes that two of the mermaids are dead –

thirty-three injured.

The nurse mermaids dress the injured in rich scented ointments and oceanic herbs.

Elena, wearing a jewelled, studded gold crown and dressed in a blue velvet cloak floats gracefully amongst the seriously injured.

She hands down kisses to each one, and touches their foreheads with a scented palm, every movement emanating rays of hope and love.

It is a moving, beautifully poignant experience.

Elena comes towards me; she speaks softly.

"The demented have been repulsed, but they have inflicted a high price. Two of my bravest warriors, Filerie and Canis, have been killed. I am deeply saddened."

Elena's face takes on a grief-stricken look.

I put my arm around her.

After a brief pause, Elena's hands gently brush my forehead in an affectionate, reassuring manner. She looks deeply into my eyes, and speaks with a deep soft voice.

"You have great depth of feeling, Adonis.

I have breathed in your beauty, and am now comforted.

"Filerie, and Canis, have attained the mermaid's highest honour – to die in battle for a noble and just cause.

I shall miss them, but soon we will be reunited.

"You must carry the battle when you return to earth.

Marah with give you light, and wisdom to touch many hearts.

She will be your counsel, and guide, for the rest of the journey."

Elena kisses me, and then exits. Enter Marah.

We sit on black mushroom chairs around an oblong table.

Marah pours me a drink.

She speaks in a confident, reassuring voice.

"I hope you are not upset at what has happened.

I'm sorry I could not be with you –

I was down below, steering the Ark.

It was very difficult – a hard battle.

But I'm glad we came through.

I know you are wondering how two of my sisters died.

Well, we are not invulnerable,

If our voice-box, which is between the ear and the neck,

Becomes crushed or damaged, we may die.

Without our voices we cannot live,

Or breathe in nature's beauty which sustains us.

"Just after the 'great catastrophe', when the world was in its Infancy, your species and mine took different evolutionary paths.

"We became angels of the sea.

"We live in two dimensions – one spiritual, the other physical.

Our physical dimension lies between those places you call Florida and Bermuda.

"Also within this area lies the spiritual dimension.

"Beings from other worlds and dimensions and our close relations, the angels of the air, fly through here.

"Your species, the dolphins and the whales are also closely related to us.

"When your people have reached a high degree of intelligence, and attained true civilisation, we will invite you to come and visit one of our cities.

"Do not worry about Filerie, and Canis.

They will find fulfilment in the world of Marisien – Mother of the Elements.

Their main task will be to warn seamen of

impending dangers. If they wish they can also live in your world." (Marah smiles)

"I have – I found great power in the human mind, but sadly it was not developed or utilised."

She pauses, and looks across.

"It is now time for the burial."

We move to the stern of the ship.

Mermaid trumpeters dressed in blue stand in a line.

Filerie and Canis lie in a heart-shaped shell coffin.

They seem to smile, and exude a radiant beauty.

Elena stands on a pedestal holding a silver staff – triangular at the top with tendrils at opposite sides.

She points the staff towards the sea and calls out in a loud voice.

Two giant sea horses emerge, followed by sea nymphs and pixies with pointed hats, who play and dance among the waves.

Trumpets sound as the coffin is lowered to the sea.

Showers of flower petals land on the coffin.

It is harnessed to the sea horses who slowly pull it away.

The mermaids form themselves into circular groups of three, hold hands, and sing a sad farewell.

Marah looks at me, and speaks softly.

"The spirit is indestructible."

The soft sea spray, wind and rain play music on my skin, and catch my soul in a cool embrace.

I lie on the hammock watching the mermaids play,

And listen to their melodic voices.

Vibrant, elegant wet legs glide past,

Evoking a feeling of deep sensuality.

Occasionally, they stop to comb their hair,

And portray a picture of youthful innocence.

Marah touches my shoulder.

"We are now coming to the land of sleep!"

The ship moves silently through a shroud-covered mist into a wide cavern.

The water changes into a deep purple colour.

Grotesque luminous-eyed ghost-like figures appear,

And then slink back into darkness.

Trees with human-type limbs, and sunken eyes, stare ominously, adding a sense of foreboding and eeriness to the surroundings.

Blackbirds, dressed as funeral undertakers,

Sit unmoved as the ship glides past.

The only sound that can be heard is the vain grasping, and rustle of ferns.

Suddenly, a giant witch appears in front of the ship.

She scoops the water with her scrawny hands and long nails.

The Ark buckles under the weight of the water, and is pushed back.

The witch slaps her thighs in glee, and cackles.

"Did ye think ye cud pass me ye pretties?

Well, ye may think again. Ahahahahaha!"

She starts throwing huge boulders which smash into the Ark, knocking some of the mermaids down. She cackles again.

"Ye shall not pass; go back from whence ye came!."

She again pushes water towards the ship. It is lifted by a huge tidal wave. Some of the mermaids fall into the water. The witch grabs them, puts them into her mouth, and starts crunching. The mermaids' blood flows over her granite chin.

"Do not look!" yells Marah.

The witch hits the Ark a mighty blow with her fist.

Then she starts blowing gusts of wind.

Marah clasps me round the waist; we go spinning in a whirlwind.

Marah's tiara begins to glow and vibrate.

Luminae and Muireadnesi run in front of us,

And hold out a blue net.

Marah lets me go, and with outstretched arms speaks in a loud tone.

"Cease, wind, cease. Be a peace, witch, peace. I am Marah, daughter of the night.

Fear cannot hold me, nor wickedness and spite.

The veil between us is the guardian of right.

So go back to the darkness, and let us pass without fight."

The witch screeches and retreats into a cave.

As the Ark approaches, the witch, in a last desperate action, flings herself on top of it. She hits the blue veil and disappears in a cloud of smoke.

Soon after we come to the end of the cavern – a ray of light shines through a small cavity.

Disaster seems imminent as the Ark heads towards the six inch wide spring. I throw myself on the deck. Amazingly, the Ark sails through without a scratch.

I rise up and look around.

We are now in a white, bright sunlit sea.

Marah's eyes glow as she speaks.

"Going through that cavern was an experience of the dark passages of the mind.

Imagination and hallucination were our hosts. The witch was a symbol of fear. Fear and discouragement are your worst enemies. You must learn to overcome them."

Marah's tiara glows again. Muireadnesi comes across.

Marah embraces Muireadnesi and exits.

I stare in wonderment at the towering mermaid. Her elegant plaited red hair and athletic beauty are beyond compare.

She speaks in a resonant tone of voice.

"I have come to teach you confidence, and to defend yourself in battle."

She invites me to attack her. As I approach, she spins round at phenomenal speed and knocks me on my back. I rise, and rush at her, but it is like chasing an elusive butterfly. She suddenly attacks me, and with fleeting light blows on the nerve points of my body, renders me defenceless.

She teaches me to use the bow and the trident spear, and to relax, and overcome fear. As I rest she brings a platter of food. The familiar honey, moss-substance, and different-coloured radish-like balls.

I eat the food, and become revitalised.

Soon I begin to move with the same athleticism and speed of the mermaids.

Trumpets sound. Marah comes across and speaks with a note of urgency.

"We are approaching the islands of Namubni. The Naibsels who live there hate all human men, and if they discover you are on board, they will attack you with great ferocity. You will have to be hidden."

The mermaids cover me with rubbery sheets, leaf and flower mats. Marah hands me a funnel-shaped object tipped by a large diamond.

"Look through this. You will see the Naibsels, but they will not see you."

I look through the periscopic object and see large numbers of scantily-clad and nude women.

Some beckon to the mermaids; others snarl abuse.

Human male skeletons pull ploughshares across the rough terrain.

Fat women riding on gelded horses whip the

skeletons, and unmercifully ride over them when they fall.

Male sex organs hang from the trees,

And babies strangled by their umbilical cords.

Beneath the trees a ghostly pair of legs walks behind a limbless, headless torso which in turn follows a male head.

A group of faceless figures of undetermined sex stand on a platform, bartering and holding fistfuls of gold, while another group bash cripples, babies and animals over the head with stone millets.

A mountain of bodies lies heaped in a deep pit.

A horde of giant rats scavenge amongst the putrefied flesh, trampling and crushing each other in their haste.

At the end of the large island a group of fat-bellied women sit.

Men crouched in foetus positions peer from the women's transparent abdomens

On a tiny island a short distance away a multitude of babies stare across, and begin to wail. The fat women cover their ears. It seems and eternity before the Ark reaches the end of the island.

The mermaids remain silent, but still in battle position.

A feathery flower petal tickles my nose inducing a loud sneeze, and blowing my cover.

A mumbling sound gradually buildings up intoan almighty roar.

A furry bridge thumps onto the Ark.

The Naibsels attack!

They swing across like pirates, and rush up the bridge.

Muireadnesi and her warriors confront them.

A fierce battle ensues.

Muireadnesi fells three of the Naibsels with one swipe – some jump on her back, and disarray her beautiful hair.

As Elena calls out orders, a Naibsel sneaks up behind her.

Luminae spears the Naibsel in the neck.

Marah rescues a tiny mermaid who is bleeding profusely from neck wounds

She carries the little mermaid under her arm to the nurse mermaids.

A group of Naibsels overpower Luminae.

She manages to swat some of them off with her tail, but as she tries to wriggle free, she is caught from behind, and a Naibsel attempts to strangle her with a leather thong.

THE MERMAID QUEEN

I pick up a sword, and instinctively rush to her aid.
Muireadnesi's teaching comes into good effect.
I swiftly kill three of the Naibsels.
The one holding Luminae releases her grip,
And springs at me like a wild cat.

We fall to the ground, and wrestle,
Incredibly strong, she gains the advantage
and fastens a leather thong around my neck.

In desperation I squeeze one of her breasts.
She grimaces with pain as I dig my fingers deep
Into the soft flesh.
I push her off when she releases her grip.

She rushes at me again. I fall backwards,
Simultaneously putting my feet on her solar plexus.
I throw her over my head into the water.
Luminae's face is badly scratched, and deathly pale.
She moans softly as I lift her onto my back,
And carry her across to the nurse mermaids.

Elena, Muireadnesi and Marah fight side by side
And force the Naibsels off the bridge.

Acid stones rain down on the other Naibsels
Clinging to the Ark.

Their skin sizzles, and they fall away like discarded leeches.

Elena rushes across to Luminae, and breaths into her mouth.
She looks at me with a sad expression
And then speaks in Luminae's ear.

"Come back, come back to life."
Luminae's eyes begin to flicker,
She gives a weak smile.

Elena strokes the injured Mermaid's hair
And speaks in a strong, sympathetic voice.

"You will not die, my brave, beautiful Luminae.
Comfort her, Adonis."

I clasp Luminae's hand in response to the command

From the mermaid queen.

Soon after, Luminae is carried below by the nurse mermaids.

Elena and I rejoin Marah and Muireadnesi,

Who have completed their rout of the Naibsels.

Suddenly a large ship appears, armed with three long, pointed battering-rams and giant catapults.

On the ship can be seen the faceless figures,

Who clench their fists, and fly a black flag

With the images of a skeleton on it.

A flotilla of smaller ships, mounted with long spears follows close behind.

They approach the Ark with great speed.

The Ark turns sharply, and tries to avoid a collision.

But it is hit in the stern; a gaping hole appears.

The mermaids rush to block it,

But are knocked back by the force of the water.

A hail of missiles thud onto the deck of the Ark,

Adding to the disarray.

Elena presses a lever, and two glass sheets arise

From opposite sides of the Ark, to form a kind of cloche.

The missiles clatter like hailstones against the glass,

But none penetrate.

The mermaids manage to seal the hole with a waxy substance fired from rectangular hand guns. The wax flows over the hole like molten lava, and hardens in seconds.

Some of the faceless figures fling themselves

On top of the Ark, and bank the glass with their fists,

But soon slide off, as the Ark turns sharply.

We are just past the island when the sky grows dark.

Some of the mermaids appear startled, and look up.

A dark cloud steadily approaches.

As it gets closer, I see the gruesome face in the middle –

Wide, fierce bloodshot eyes, and a shark-like mouth.

As the cloud swirls, the features become elongated and distorted.

The protective glass sheets tremble, and then descend.

Elena calls out instructions to Marah.

She rushed over, and speaks urgently.

"It is 'The Cloud of Death';

Our main defence system is malfunctioning.

Photosynthetic energisers have broken down.

Unicellular light reactors have become neutralised.

Take this."

Marah hands me a silky rope fastened to a metal clasp.

"In the belly of the Ark you will find a square metal box.

Put the clasp into the slot in the metal box,,

And tie the rope around your waist.

That way you will be safe."

As we rush towards the entrance to the hold, the ship stalls, and the sea begins to heave 0 knocking us off-balance.

"Hang on to me," Marah shouts.

I clasp her tightly, and look up.

An incredible sight meets my gaze.

The 'death cloud' has now become a huge wall of sea, trapping the Ark on all sides.

The sky seems to fall as the blanket comes crashing down.

Marah and I are swept mercilessly into the angry sea,

And tossed about like flies.

Her hand gradually slips away from me. I lose consciousness…

I awaken to find myself being carried in an open coffin

By four mermaids.

The coffin is transferred to four familiar-looking men who carry it through golden gates into a cemetery.

I realise the men are relatives, and friends long deceased.

A minister stands reading from a bible.

He puts an hour-glass into the coffin,

And speaks in a soft voice.

"The Kingdom of Heaven is likened to a grain of sand.

See how swiftly it passes. Your hour has not yet come."

As the coffin is lovwered into the grave,

Four banshees comb their hair and wail,

I want to escape, but find I cannot move.

My body is reduced to a paralytic state,

And floats from side to side.

A demon laughs mockingly, and taunts me, saying.

"There is no light, only darkness."

You are a dupe, full of elupe.

There is no hope – no hope.

You are not well; give me your soul to sell.

Come to Hell – Let's go to Hell."

Prayers to St Michael. Archangel, that I learned at school come to mind. I begin to say them.

The demon angrily tries to shout me down, but gradually disappears.

Sunlight caresses my brow, and dazzles my eyes.

I hear the sound of a horn, repeating intermittently and getting louder each time.

The rhythmical floating sensation is still present in my body.

Human voices bring an air of reality. A pair of craggy hands grab, and lift me. I black out

When I regain consciousness, I am lying in a bed in a ship's cabin.

Beside the bed on a small table is a half-bottle of whiskey and two miniature Greco-Roman statues.

I rise up slightly, and hold my throbbing 'lead head'.

The door knocks, and a tubby bearded chap wearing a blazer and a peaked cap enters.

He speaks with a West Country accent.

"Hello, matey; I'm Captain Jones. Are ye alright?"

I nod, and clasp, his outstretched hand.

"It's a miracle ye survived.

Yer ship, 'The Adonis' went down in a fierce storm about three months ago."

The captain pauses, his face takes on a pensive expression as he tugs gently at his beard.

"We picked up another survivor. I think she said her name was Maria. Did ye know her?"

I stare at the Captain with a mixture of surprise and shock.

The Captain's face takes on a sad expression.

"Poor girl; the ordeal must have been too much for her.

Sad to say, she jumped over the side,

the day after we picked her up.

We searched everywhere, but couldn't find her.

She was a nice girl."

The Captain pauses again.

"At least we can be consoled that ye survived.

I'm still mystified as to how ye did it.

I think ye must have eaten seaweed.

When we found ye there was seaweed

Or a moss thing in your mouth.

My bosun removed it, and threw it into the water."

The Captain gives a little laugh.

"You know he swore blind

That a lady with golden hair came up out of the sea, and picked it up, and then waved goodbye.

Can you believe that?"

I nodded, and smiled.

The Captain stared in surprise,

Shook his head disbelievingly. And then walked away.

If only he knew…

Printed in Great Britain
by Amazon